JIM BRICKMAN

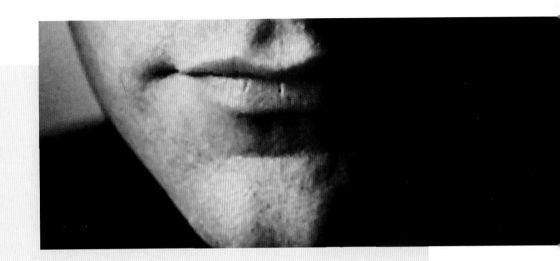

NO WORDS

Artwork and Photography © 1994 Windham Hill Records
Album Photography: Jeff Sedlik

Project Manager: Jeannette DeLisa
Art Layout: Ken Rehm

C O N T E N T S

ROCKET TO THE MOON

Composed by
JIM BRICKMAN

Rocket to the Moon - 6 - 1
PF9631

8

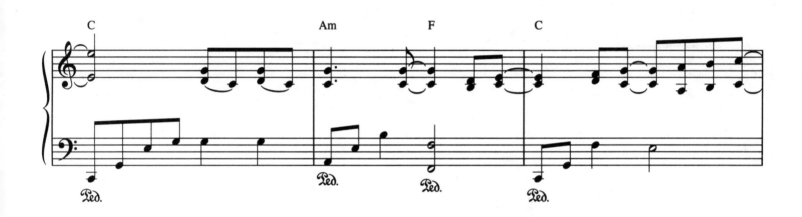

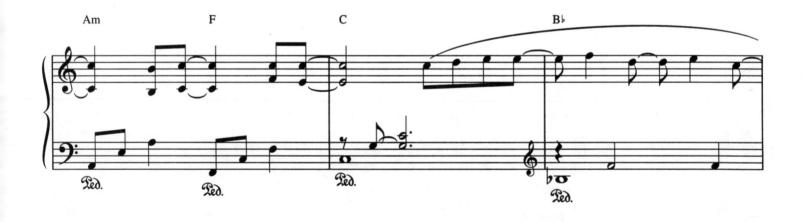

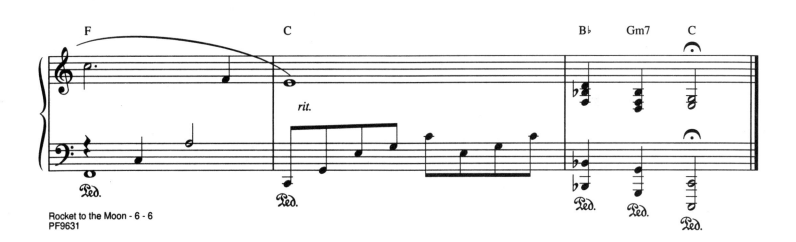

Rocket to the Moon - 6 - 6
PF9631

SHAKER LAKES

Composed by
JIM BRICKMAN

OPEN DOORS

Composed by
JIM BRICKMAN

Slowly and expressively (♩. = ca.52)

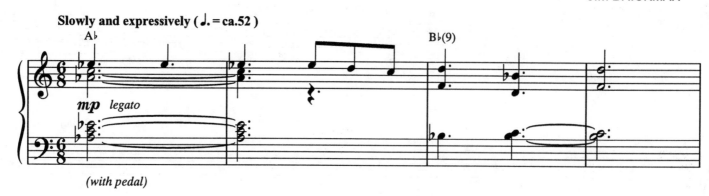

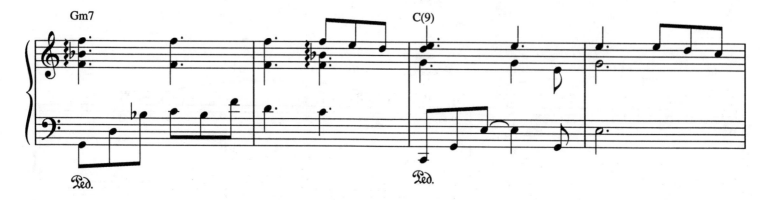

Open Doors - 5 - 1
PF9631

I SAID... YOU SAID

Composed by
JIM BRICKMAN

I Said... You Said - 5 - 1
PF9631

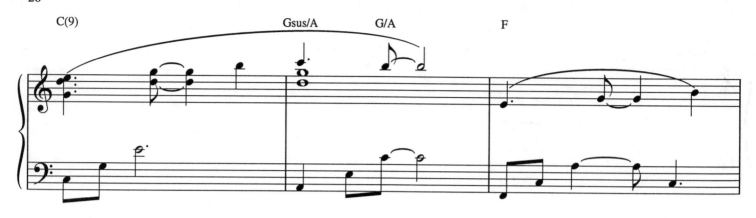

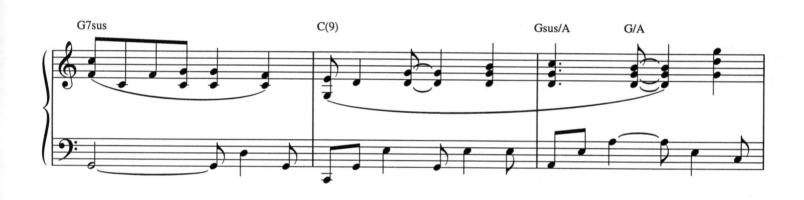

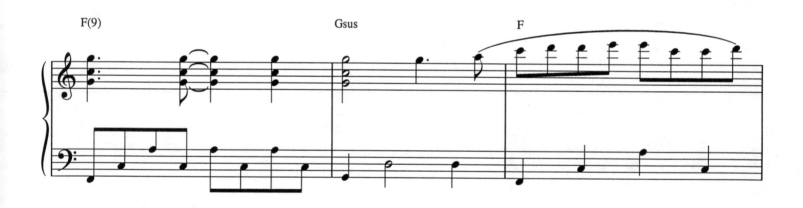

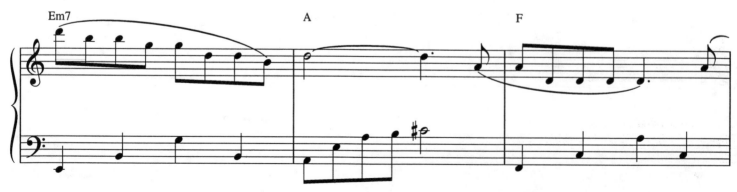

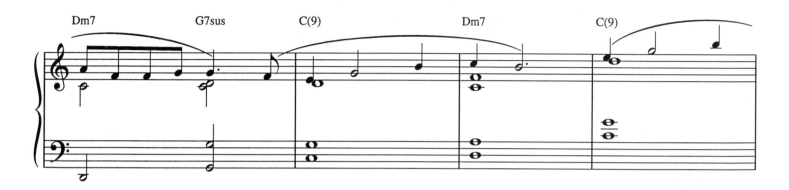

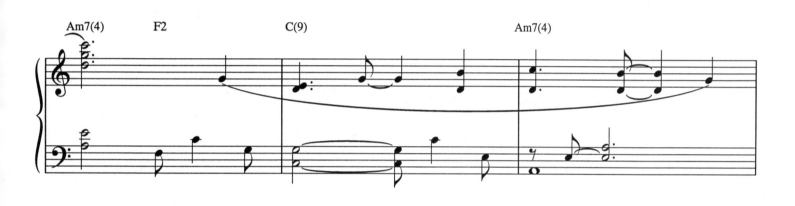

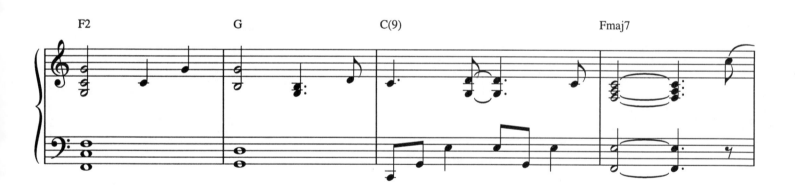

WANDERLUST

Composed by
JIM BRICKMAN

32

HEARTLAND

Composed by
JIM BRICKMAN and
ELLEN WOHL

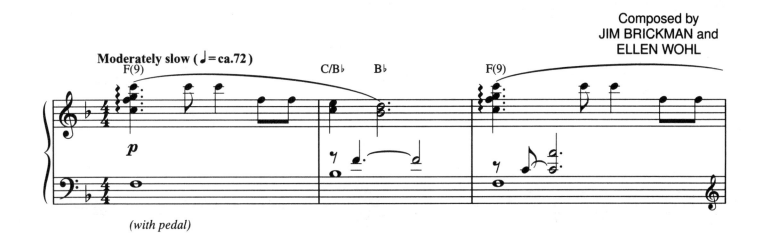

(with pedal)

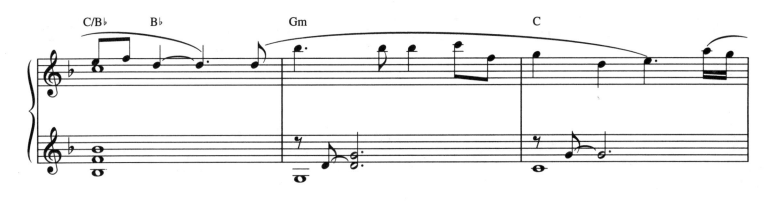

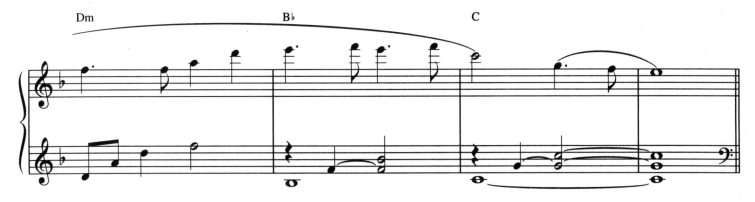

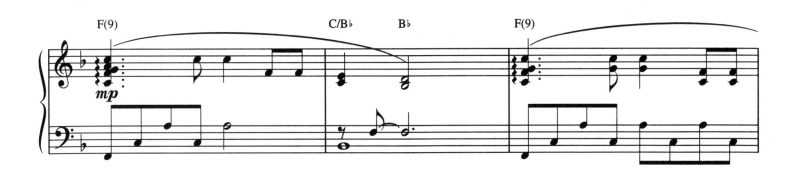

Heartland - 4 - 1
PF9631

BORDERS

Composed by
JIM BRICKMAN

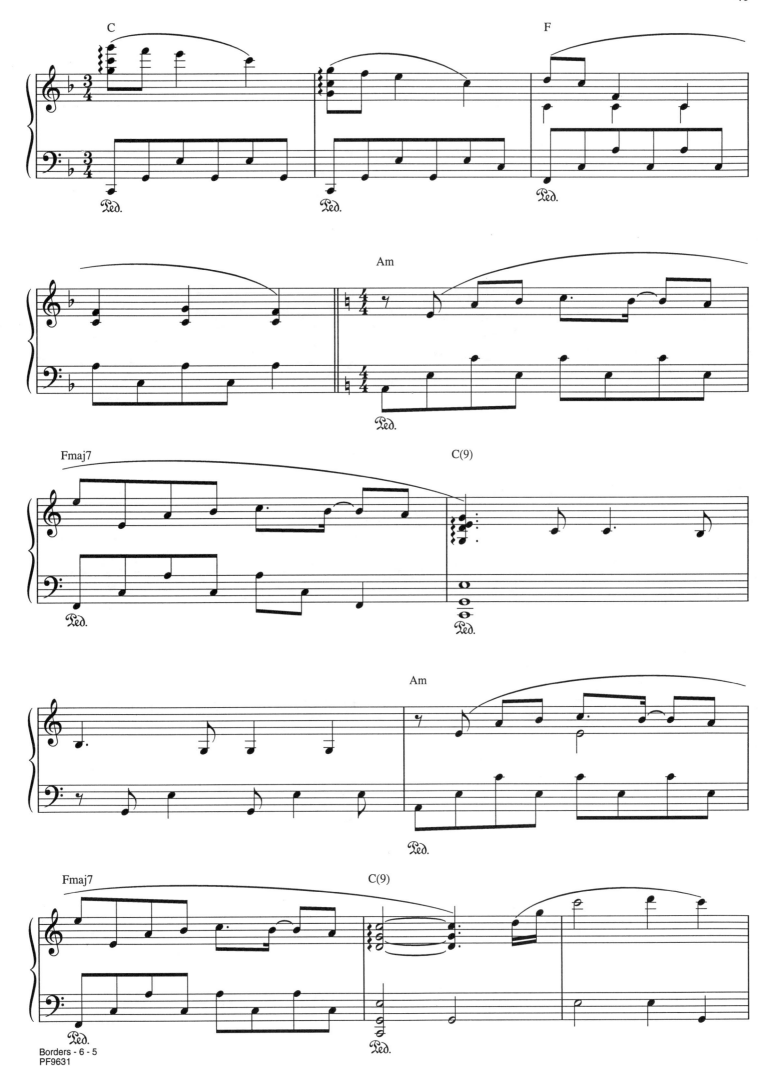

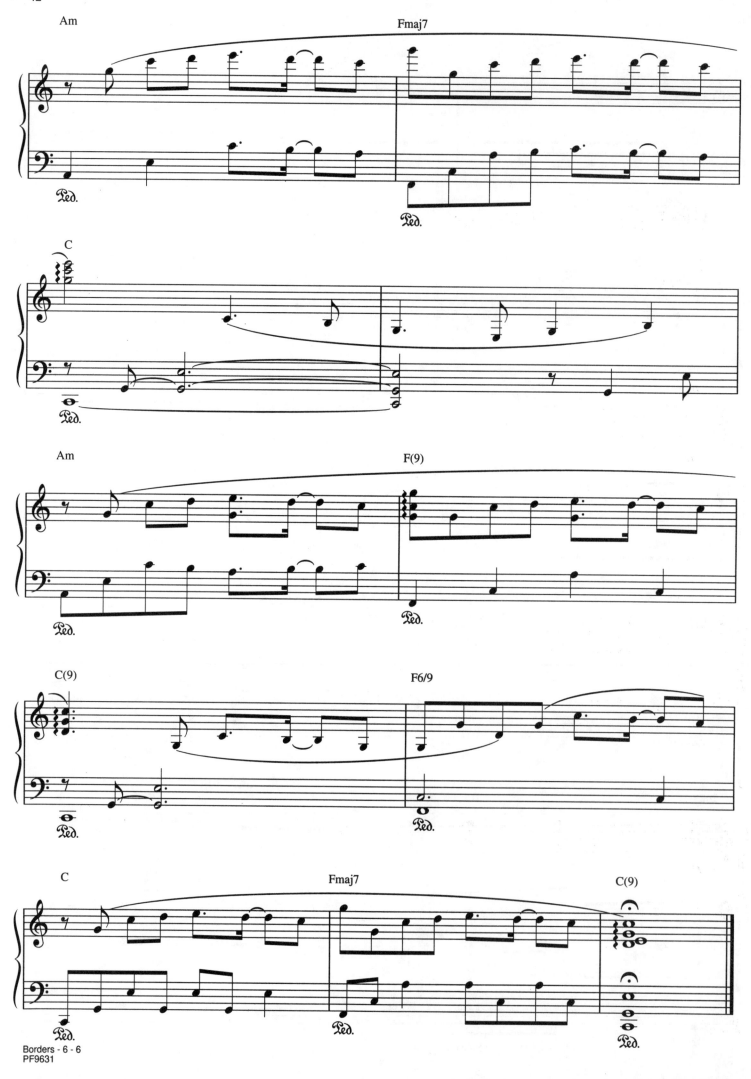

STILL

Composed by
JIM BRICKMAN

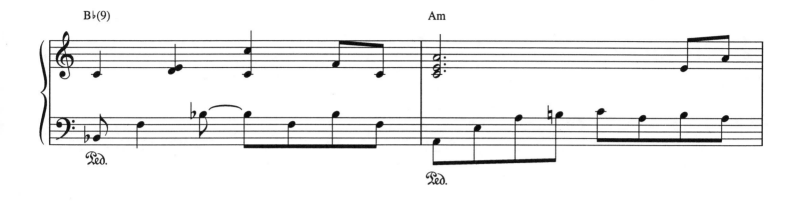

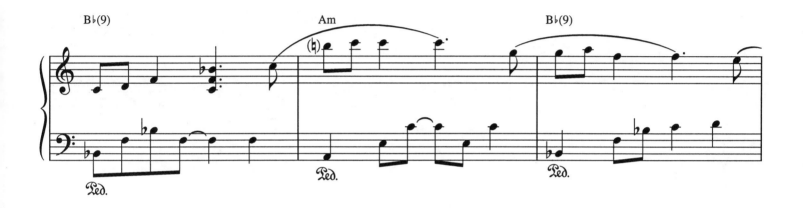

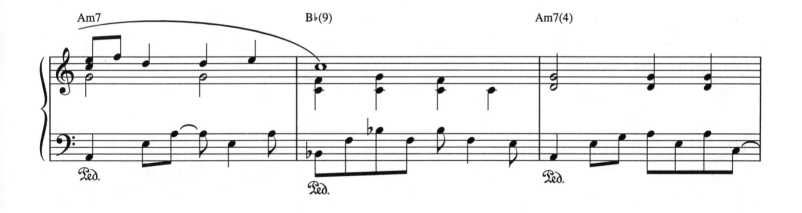

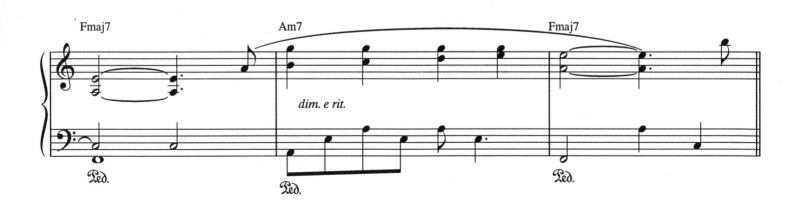

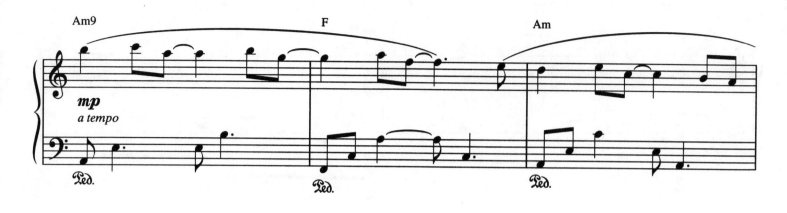

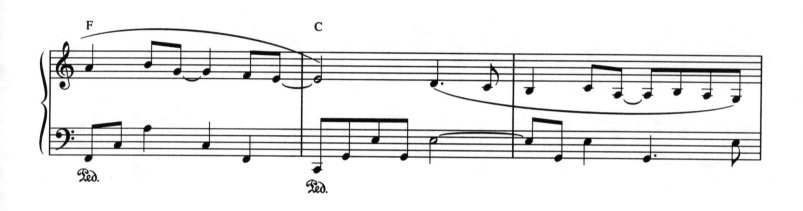

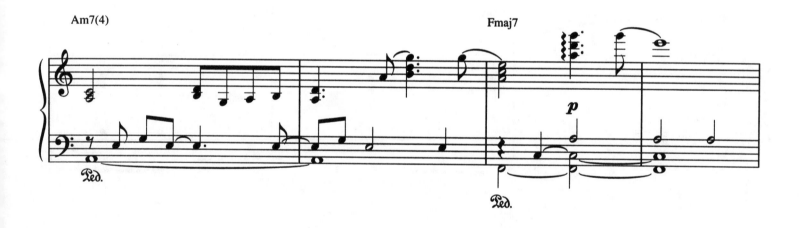

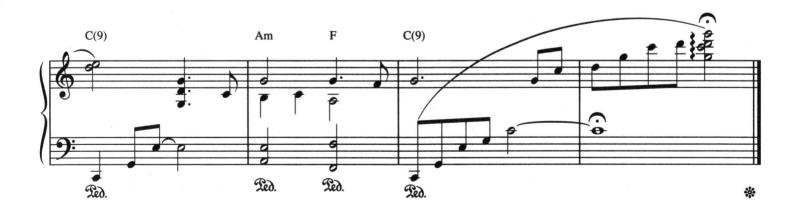

AMERICAN DREAM

Composed by
JIM BRICKMAN

BLUE

Composed by
JIM BRICKMAN

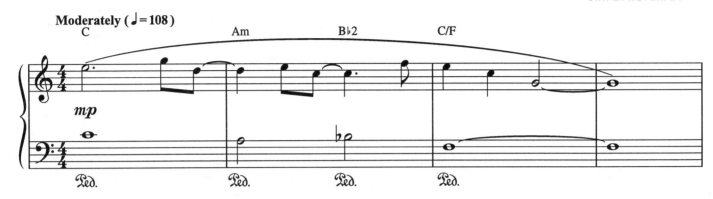

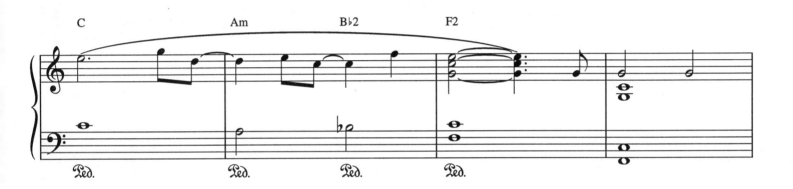

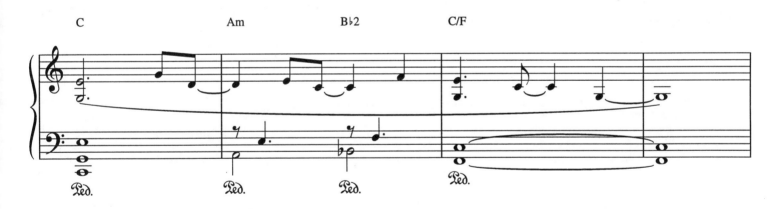

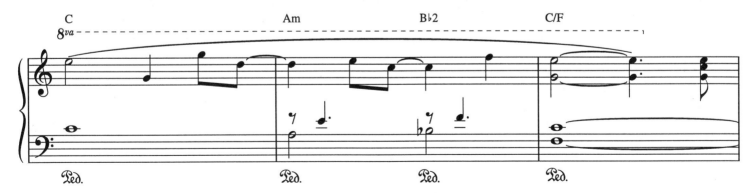

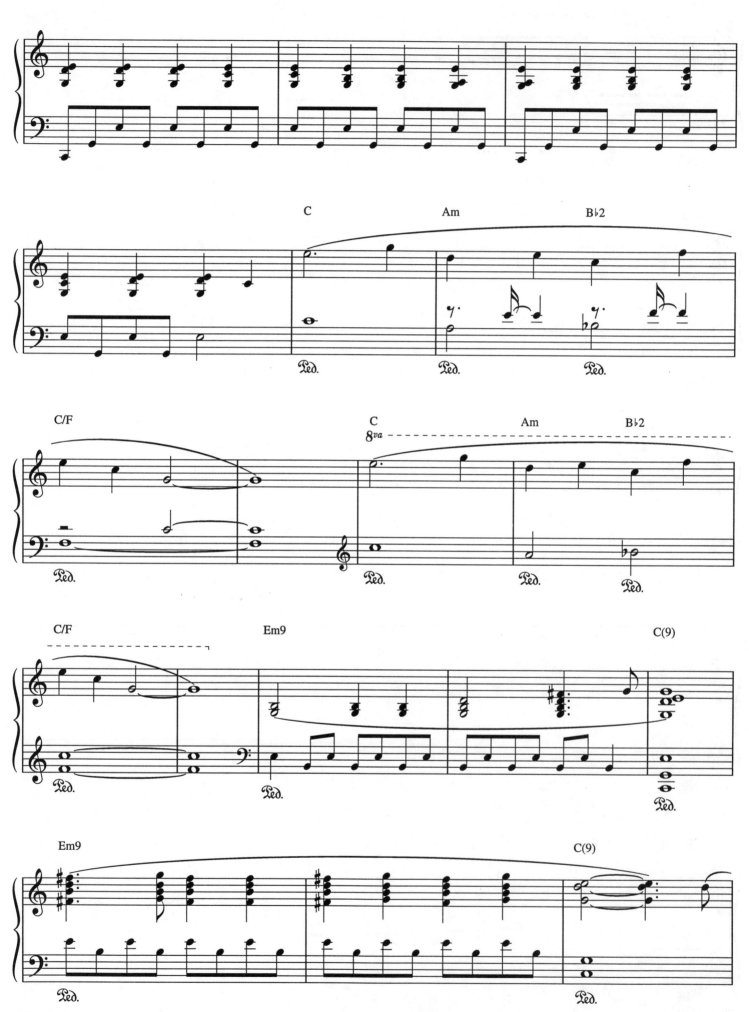

OLD TIMES

Composed by
JIM BRICKMAN and
ELLEN WOHL

Old Times - 5 - 1
PF9631

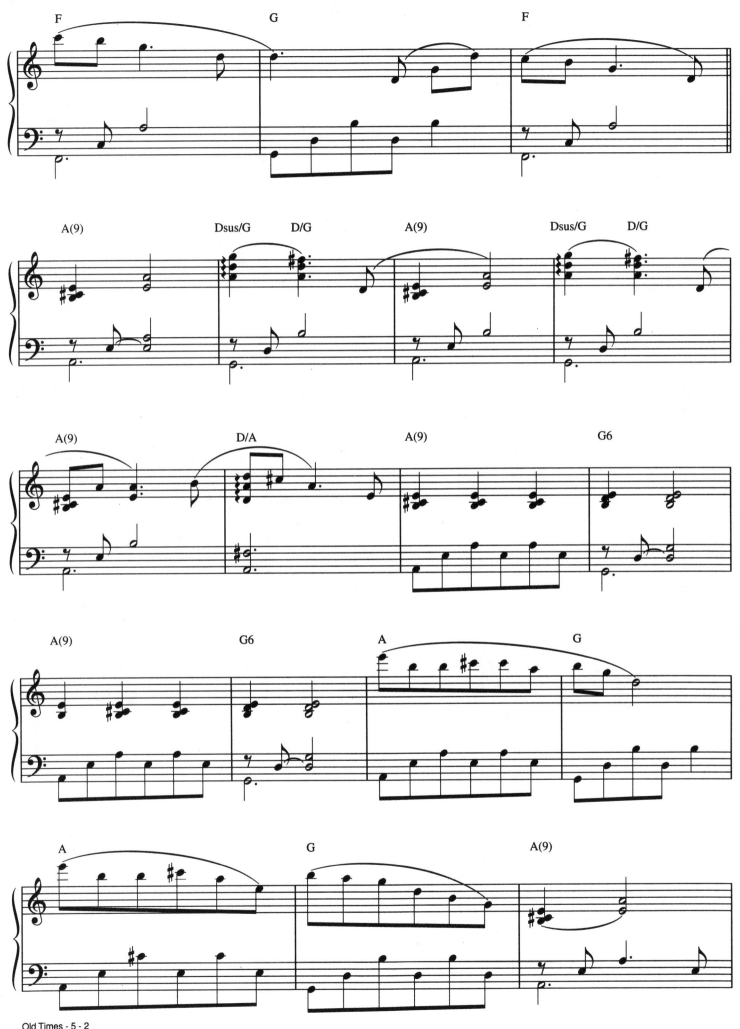

SO LONG

Composed by
JIM BRICKMAN

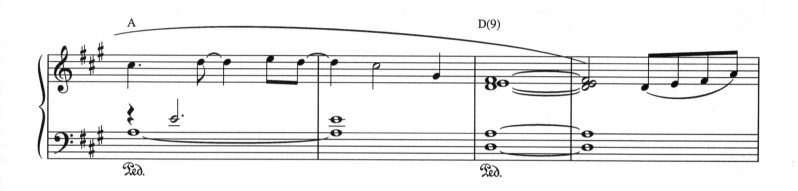

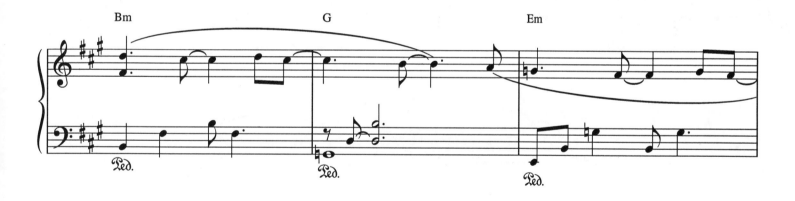

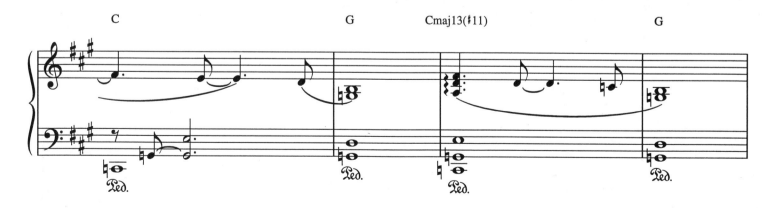

So Long - 7 - 1
PF9631

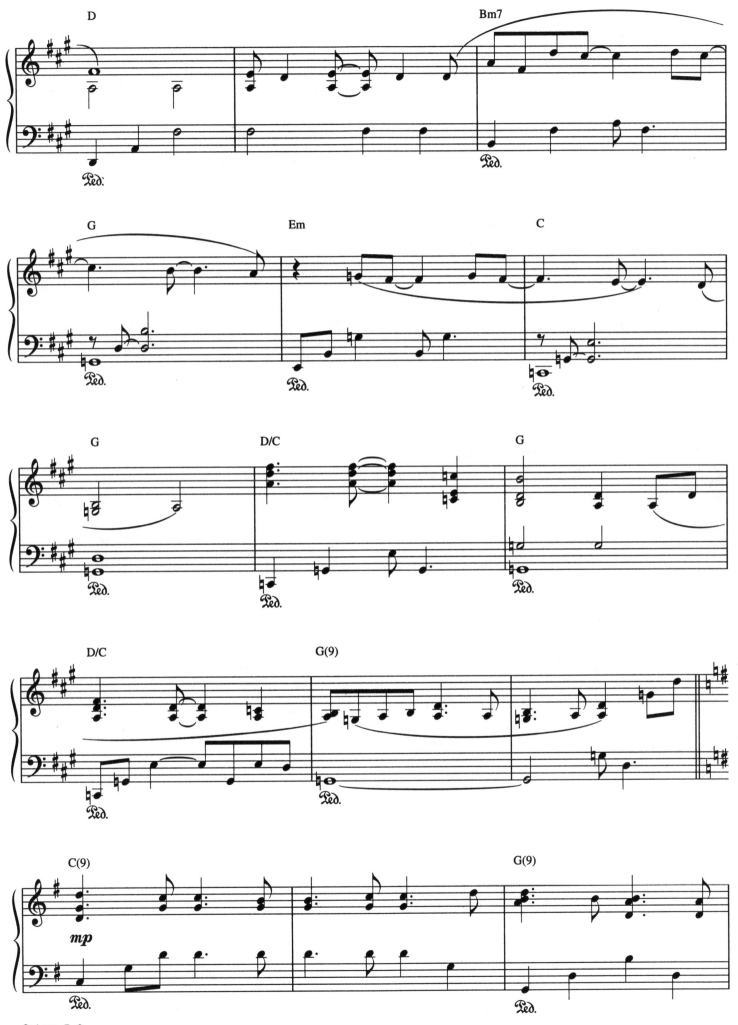

WE MET TODAY

Composed by
JIM BRICKMAN

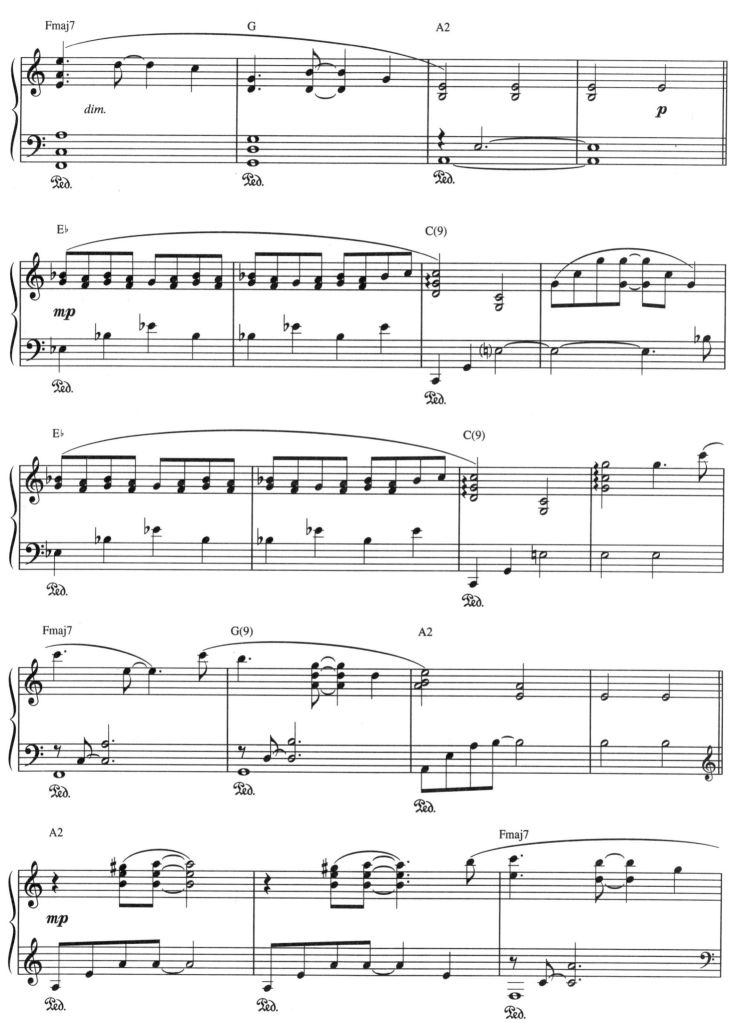

JIM BRICKMAN

BIOGRAPHY

Welcome to *No Words*. One Person On One Piano. No band. No vocals. No lofty pretensions. No kidding.

No Words was the album debut of pianist **Jim Brickman,** an award-winning composer and performer.

Armed with a wealth of inviting compositions, this uniquely romantic work paved the way for the future of solo piano. As evidenced on *No Words,* Brickman's gentle song-like instrumentals favor warm melodies and memorable choruses. Each tune is highly lyrical, making words unnecessary. Brickman's playing freely emotes, but does not resemble free-form jazz. He is a classically-trained performer accustomed to conservatory recitals, yet his music is not rigidly formal. It immediately sounds familiar, and yet . . .

If it's hard to put a finger on Brickman's style, that's because we honestly have not heard anything like it before. "I realize that what I'm doing is very unusual: solo piano instrumental pop music," says the personable musician who was the first new solo pianist signed to Windham Hill Records in seven years. "The great thing about it, and the reason I believe in it so strongly, is that it's exposing a much greater audience to instrumental music. Solo piano shouldn't have to be so esoteric that it's out of reach for the average listener."

Brickman admits that he has always been "a break-the-rules kind of guy." At the Cleveland Institute of Music, the classical composition and performance student was the black sheep of the conservatory. "Everybody was putting their studies to use in a very classical sense, but I was applying it toward the mainstream," he says. "That's what came naturally to me . . . pop songwriting."

While residing in the campus dormitory, the 19-year-old committed musical sacrilege by launching his professional career . . . as a commercial jingle writer. As founder and president of The Brickman Arrangement -- the production company based in Los Angeles -- he has since become known as the composer of some of the best-known music on radio and TV. He has created music for McDonald's, 7-Up, Sony, G.E., Ohio Lottery and Disney.

In the advertising world, his back-to-basics, Tin Pan Alley sensibilities are practically legendary. "It's very real. It's rooted in the basics of the instrument," enthuses the piano man who still plays the same beat-up Yamaha upright he's had since he was ten. "It's really like the starving-artist syndrome in that it keeps me grounded. If I'm set up in a beautiful studio with a stellar grand piano, I can't write. The only thing that jingle-writing and my songwriting have in common is that they both affect people," he explains. "I'm always striving to write dramatic hooks that people will remember, and to write melodies that sound like you've heard them before. I want my music to be familiar so that it's accessible."

Hence *No Words*' peaceful yet chordally-complex "Shaker Lakes," that paints a tone poem about his favorite childhood retreat in suburban Cleveland. The sonic travels of "Wanderlust" underscore Brickman's incessant desire to explore new things. The loping waltz of "Open Doors" welcomes listeners inside and makes them feel at home. But perhaps most memorable is the album's opening piece: the romantic "Rocket To The Moon." Jim says, "It's about freedom and letting go, and it's the song I let go the most on." Appropriately, it's also the first song that he wrote and recorded for *No Words*. "I went in the studio and just let loose," he recalls. "We were supposed to be testing the microphone sound, but by the end I said, 'I hope you got that,' because that was it. I really believe in that: the impulse and the freedom of not consciously knowing you're performing."

"Hopefully, more than anything else, *No Words* is *nice*," he concludes. "And if *nice* becomes the most appropriate adjective for my music, that's fine with me. Everybody has a place in their music collection for something nice."

OTHER WINDHAM HILL RELEASES BY OR FEATURING

JIM BRICKMAN

INCLUDE:

NO WORDS • PIANO SAMPLER 2 • A WINTER SOLSTICE V
WINDHAM HILL SAMPLER 1996

JIM BRICKMAN would like to invite you to be on his Mailing List to receive information about concert schedules, merchandise and upcoming releases. Please fill out the coupon below and mail to:

JIM BRICKMAN
c/o EDGE MANAGEMENT
11288 VENTURA BLVD. SUITE 606
STUDIO CITY, CA 91604

(818) 508-8400 **phone**
(818) 508-8444 **fax**

or

E-Mail us at BrickPiano@AOL.com.
Also, please visit our current Internet Site on the Worldwide Web at WINDHAM.com.

Cut Along Here ✄

NAME_____

ADDRESS_____

CITY_____ **STATE**_____ **ZIP**_____

SEX: M___ F___ **E-Mail**_____

*I first heard about Jim Brickman's music*_____

No Words